10 Wise & Wonderful Stories for Children

Celebrating Holidays & Holy Days

Sr. M. Valerie Schneider, SND

TWENTY THIRD 23rd
PUBLICATIONS

Illustrated by Robert Veal

Twenty-Third Publications
A Division of Bayard
One Montauk Avenue, Suite 200
New London, CT 06320
(860) 437-3012 or (800) 321-0411
www.23rdpublications.com

ISBN 978-1-58595-614-2
Library of Congress Catalog Card Number: 2006939676
Printed in the U.S.A.

Contents

Introduction

Jesus was a great storyteller. Don't you wish you could have sat on the hillside while Jesus told his parables or preached his Sermon on the Mount? Had you been a child during Jesus' public life, imagine yourself sitting in Jesus' lap, receiving his blessing, and begging for "just one more story, Jesus, one more!"

The ten stories in this book cannot compete with the stories of Jesus, but they may in some way help "break open the Scriptures" for children.

Each chapter includes

- an introduction,
- a Scripture passage with questions,
- a child's story with questions,
- a quiet prayer experience,
- suggested activities.

Engaging and practical, the lessons are valuable resources for both parochial schools and religious education programs.

Using Your Creativity

As with any part of your religion session, feel free to employ your own creativity in adapting and using these story-lessons with your own learners. You may choose to use them in their entirety or choose only certain parts. You might divide the lesson over two sessions. In a parochial school setting the child's story could become part of a language arts class, and the activities could be used as part of an art class, thus integrating religion with other disciplines.

With younger children you might choose to use a children's Bible for reading the Scripture passages. Instead of reading the fictional stories, you can tell them in your own words or you can have older children act them out. For some lessons you may prefer to use the meditation as the opening prayer.

An important aspect to these stories is to help your learners grasp the lesson hidden in them in a way that is age appropriate. With younger children, asking basic, factual questions about the story or having them retell it in their own words is a good way to review and reinforce the lesson. Older children are able to delve a little deeper and can discuss the choices of the characters in a story and why a choice is good or not. The activities can assist in assimilating the message in an enjoyable way. Again, they are a starting point for your creativity.

Conclusion

My hope is that the fictional stories, linked to the Scripture passages, will add to the teacher's creative approach for holydays, feast days like St. Patrick's Day, and special holidays such as Presidents' Day. With some adaptation, the lessons can be used almost any day of the year.

May these stories be a blessing for you and for those you teach. Through them may your learners be encouraged to bless our loving God.

St. Francis's Pet Parade

Saint Francis is well known for many things. Traditionally he was the first person to arrange a Christmas manger scene. He was known for giving up his wealth to become poor like Jesus. Other men and women followed his example and became known as Franciscan priests, sisters, and brothers.

Francis is also known for his love of creation. In fact, he wrote a famous, lovely poem about creation. In it he calls the sun, moon, stars, trees, and so on his sisters and brothers. Stories are told of his care for animals. That is why he is often shown surrounded by animals. In our story we will read about a pet parade in honor of Saint Francis.

The Scripture Reading

People were bringing little children to Jesus in order that he might touch them; and the disciples spoke sternly to them. But when Jesus saw this, he was indignant and said to them, "Let the little children come to me; do not stop them; for it is to such as these that the kingdom of God belongs. Truly I tell you, whoever does not receive the kingdom of God as a little child will never enter it." And he took them up in his arms, laid his hands on them, and blessed them. (Mark 10:13–16)

Understanding the Bible Story

1. Why did people bring their children to Jesus?

2. Why did the disciples scold them?

3. Did Jesus want to be with the children?

4. Who will be in the kingdom of heaven?

5. How did Jesus bless the children? What is a blessing?

Meditation

Imagine that you are with your parents, who see Jesus sitting near a tree. Picture Jesus resting there. Your parents think it is a good time to have Jesus bless you. They take you to Jesus and tell him your name. How do you feel? Jesus reaches out to pull you onto his lap. He puts his hand on your head and says a blessing. Hear what Jesus says. (*pause*) Jesus then asks you to tell him about anything you'd like to talk about. Share with him whatever is in your heart. (*Pause in silence.*)

ST. FRANCIS'S PET PARADE

Before reading the story tell the children that they will be asked to give their name and the name of their pet(s)—if they have any—during the story.

P.J., Gavin's pet cat, licked his black paws and stretched his jet-black body in the sun. He sensed that today was a special day. Yes, P.J. remembered that the boy Gavin had said that today was October 4, the feast of Saint Francis of Assisi. There would be a pet parade at school!

Practicing his strutting, P.J. almost tripped over Elegant, Scott's golden retriever. Thirteen-year-old Scott loved Elegant and was proud of his dog. Elegant opened her eyes, blinked at P.J., and asked, "What do you think you're doing? Watch where you are walking!"

"Now that you're awake, you had better get ready. Don't you remember? Gavin and Scott told us today is the feast of Saint Francis. There will be a pet parade!"

Elegant jumped up, wagged her tail, and shook her long golden body. The bright sun glistened on her golden fur. Elegant looked beautiful. P.J. realized he had no chance to win a pet parade if Elegant was also a contestant. For the first time in his life P.J. was jealous.

He didn't like the feeling; jealousy made him feel cunning and sly. He imagined himself a big cat like a leopard—yes, a leopard! He liked imagining he was really big. He felt so big that he knew he could beat Elegant and any other pet in the parade. But he would have to plan.

Meanwhile, Scott and Gavin raced to the bathroom. When their mother called them, neither one said, "Ah, Mom! Do I have to get up?" Even before their eyes were completely open, both of them remembered, "Today's the day! The pet parade!"

Ever since the first day of school when their principal, Sister Mary Ellen, had announced the pet parade, they had been preparing. Each day the two boys groomed their pets with special care. Every day they measured out just the right amount of food. They practiced walking in a circle with their pets on a leash and made sure P.J. and Elegant knew when to stop.

Even though the parade was on a Saturday, Scott and Gavin were eager to get to school. The day before, the eighth graders had roped off a section of the playground. They put up streamers and signs and met with Father John to write a prayer of blessing.

As Scott and Gavin jumped out of the car, they saw that many other children were gathering with their pets.

[At this point in the story, allow the children to pretend they are part of the group gathering at the school. All may take turns to say their name and their pet's name and what it is; for example, "I'm Meghan, and I brought my pet turtle named Oscar."]

Over the excited sounds of the children, Father John announced on the microphone, "Children, line up behind the balloon arch."

P.J. meowed and pushed against Gavin's leg. "Hurry up!" he wanted to tell Gavin. P.J. wanted to be the first one. But Gavin wasn't hurrying. He was only in first grade and he didn't know what to do. He had never seen a Saint Francis parade. Fortunately, Sister Ellen told the youngest children to get in line first and helped them get ready. The first graders would lead the parade, followed by the second graders, and so on.

"Great!" P.J. thought. "I'll be seen first! I'll make a wonderful first impression. By the time Scott comes through with the other eighth graders, Elegant will be just one of many pets. No one will even notice her." With those thoughts, P.J. purred contentedly and stood proudly, tail and neck high in the air, waiting for the signal to walk around the ring. P.J. imagined himself looking just like a panther.

Gavin and P.J. led the parade. There were black cats, yellow cats, gray and striped cats. The dogs included cocker spaniels, bull dogs, terriers, mutts, and others. Elegant looked just too elegant, P.J. thought with envy. One third grader had a pet goat, and a

fourth grader had a toad. A llama in the sixth-grade section loomed over the other animals, laughing at the fun. A seventh grader tugged at a stubborn ostrich. "Who allowed an ostrich to be part of the pet parade?" thought P.J. "This isn't supposed to be a zoo!" P.J. was very jealous. Finally, the eighth graders started out, and Elegant had her chance to join the parade.

All the animals had paraded once around the ring. P.J. sat very tall and straight as he waited for the ribbons to be awarded. But nothing happened. P.J. glanced around, left and right, left and right. He couldn't see any judges!

Where were they? Instead he saw Father John with a leafy twig. Beside him walked a sixth-grade girl carrying a bowl of water. "What's this?" thought P.J. "That's the fanciest water bowl I've ever seen! Which animal gets to drink from that?"

Father John said, "Children, hold your pets still now. We are going to pray." Father then extended his hand over the bowl and prayed, "God, our good Father, who has given us all creation, bless this water, the work of your hands. With this water we will bless the wonders of your creation and especially these fine pets.

6

As drops of water fall on the children and their pets, bless each child and pet with good health and a happy life. O God, fill each child with gratitude for the works of creation and respect for all you have made in our universe. Help them be like Saint Francis, who cared for every creature and saw in everything your mighty power and loving hand. We ask this through Jesus, our Brother, in the unity of the Holy Spirit. Amen." Then Father John dipped the leafy branch into the bowl and sprinkled water over every pet and child.

Splash! P.J. hated water! Water was on his back, in his eyes, and settling in a little pool under his paws. He shook himself, then stuck out his tongue to wipe himself off. P.J. sputtered, "What's the meaning of this? I wanted a ribbon. I deserve a ribbon. I was the best-looking cat in the parade. And all I got was drenched!" P.J. was angry.

The parade disbanded, and all the children rushed toward the refreshment table. Mothers poured orange juice and passed out doughnuts. Kids began to gather at picnic tables and on the ground. They had been waiting for this day since the first day of school. It had been so much fun that it was worth the wait. Father John and Sister Ellen came around to the groups to admire the pets and to tell the children how well they had cared for them. After a while, moms, dads, and grandparents finished their coffee and rounded up their children. Pets were coaxed back into their cages.

"See you next year on the feast of Saint Francis!" Father John called out.

"Good-bye, Father!" the children waved.

As they buckled their seat belts, Gavin said to Scott, "That sure was fun! I want to come next year!"

Scott replied, "See, I told you it would be fun. Too bad this is my last year at this school." Gavin felt a little pang in his heart, remembering that he would be in the same school as his older brother for only one more year.

In the back of the van, Elegant said to P.J., "I feel so blessed. Every year we receive the blessing on Saint Francis Day, and God has always protected me. I've had close calls, but I've never been hit by a car and I've never been seriously sick."

P.J. was angry. "Who cares about the blessing? I wanted a ribbon. I was the finest cat in the parade!"

Elegant put her paw on top of P.J.'s and said, "Blessings are better than ribbons. What do ribbons do? They hang on a wall or they're placed in a drawer. After a while, no one even pays attention to ribbons. But a blessing makes you a better cat. With a blessing God watches over you. If you do become sick or injured, a blessing will help you bear the pain patiently."

"But I led the parade! Shouldn't that count for something?"

Elegant was very patient and sensitive to P.J.'s feelings, but she wasn't going to let him whine forever. "You looked wonderful leading the parade. I was very proud to call you my friend and I was very happy for Gavin. You know how much we love Gavin, don't you?

P.J., tell me. Did I look any less elegant when I was last in the parade?"

P.J. thought, then replied, "No, you looked wonderful, Elegant. You were like...you were like saving the best until last!" Suddenly P.J. realized that it was true: ribbons were nice, but blessings were better.

P.J. admitted, "I see what you mean. Who we are is better than where we are."

Elegant smiled. "Do you remember Father John's prayer about being God's creatures?"

"Yes," P.J. said.

"Isn't it great to know that God made only one P.J. and only one Elegant? We are the best we can be. That's better than any ribbon. We already know that we're #1 in God's eyes. Too bad we don't come with designer labels. Mine would say, 'God's Creation. Made in heaven.'"

P.J. agreed and then added, "It's time for my cat nap." P.J. tucked his tail under his chin and shut his eyes. Elegant yawned, too. Soon little cat snores and big dog snores seemed to say to anyone who might be listening, "I like who I am. I'm made by God."

Understanding the Story

1. What are some things P.J. the cat did that he should not have done?
2. What part of the blessing didn't P.J. like?
3. Why did Father John use water?
4. What did Father John pray?
5. Tell how Elegant explained that blessings are better than ribbons.

Suggested Activities

1. As a class draw a mural of Saint Francis surrounded by animals.
2. Instruct the children to draw a picture of Jesus blessing children.

They can put themselves in the picture. How would they feel?

3. Have the learners make paper figures or sock puppets of the animals in the story "St. Francis's Pet Parade." They can attach the paper figures to sticks to move them around. Then use the puppets to act out their own version of the story.

4. Have a parade in which each child holds up a picture of their pet or of a beautiful scene of creation. As the children walk, they can say, "Praise God for creation!" Or they might sing a song of praise that they know.

Spooktacular Magnet

HALLOWEEN

ALL SAINTS
DAY

SAINTS

LEAD PEOPLE
TO GOD

Halloween is the "holy evening" before All Saints Day. November 1 is the day on which we honor all the persons in heaven, those who have been named saints and those who have not. This could include relatives, friends, and neighbors who have died. How did all these people get to heaven? They loved God above all, prayed, and did good deeds, like giving food to the hungry and clothes to people who have none. Today we will read stories about doing good things for others. What we do for others we do for God.

The Scripture Reading

Before reading this long passage, give children parts to dramatize: being hungry and thirsty, being in need of clothing or comfort, welcoming the stranger, visiting the sick, and so on. Practice the pantomime and tell the children to listen for their part.

Jesus said, "When the Son of Man comes in his glory, and all the angels with him, then he will sit on the throne of his glory. All the nations will be gathered

9

before him, and he will separate people one from another as a shepherd separates the sheep from the goats, and he will put the sheep at his right hand and the goats at the left. Then the king will say to those at his right hand, 'Come, you that are blessed by my Father, inherit the kingdom prepared for you from the foundation of the world; for I was hungry and you gave me food, I was thirsty and you gave me something to drink, I was a stranger and you welcomed me, I was naked and you gave me clothing, I was sick and you took care of me, I was in prison and you visited me.' Then the righteous will answer him, 'Lord, when was it that we saw you hungry and gave you food, or thirsty and gave you something to drink? And when was it that we saw you a stranger and welcomed you, or naked and gave you clothing? And when was it that we saw you sick or in prison and visited you?' And the king will answer them, 'Truly I tell you, just as you did it to one of the least of these who are members of my family, you did it to me.'" (Matthew 25:31–40)

Understanding the Bible Story

1. What is meant by "judgment"?
2. What good deeds did the sheep do?
3. Who are the needy people?
4. From this story what do we learn about living in heaven forever?
5. All of God's children are our brothers and sisters. Name some ways you can feed your hungry sisters and brothers or perform other works of mercy.

Meditation

Pretend you are watching television. You see pictures of hungry people, homeless people, people who need clothes and medicine. Pretend Jesus sits beside you as you're watching TV. What does Jesus say to you about the pictures you see of needy people? (*pause*) What do you want to say to Jesus about the needy people? (*pause*) Tell Jesus that when you see sisters and brothers in need you will remember his words—that what you do for them, you do for Jesus. (*pause*) Now "turn off" the television. (*Pause in silence.*)

SPOOKTACULAR MAGNET

Before reading the story ask the children to say "In God's eyes we're the best" whenever the reader makes a certain movement. The asterisk (*) in the story indicates when "In God's eyes we're the best" should be said.

Once upon a time long ago—as long ago as the first refrigerators found their way into people's houses—everything inside, attached to, and on top of refrigerators could talk at midnight on October 31, Halloween. Since those objects could talk only one night of the whole year, you'd think that they would discuss really important things like politics and prayer, sunrises and sunsets, and family and friends. But they didn't. Instead they argued.

They argued about which of them was the most important.

The carrots said, "We are the most important. Our brilliantly-colored vitamins help people see better."*

The potatoes said, "Oh, come on! Don't you know that everyone loves mashed potatoes? We're really comfort food, especially when we're smothered in butter and gravy."*

"That's right!" the butter and gravy chimed in.

The milk declared, "Without me people wouldn't have strong bones and teeth. People couldn't eat any of the rest of you without milk to make

their teeth strong. And they certainly couldn't go to the grocery store if they didn't have strong bones."*

The punch and fruit drinks and soda were quite pompous and proud. "We are the life of the party," they boasted.*

The pork chops and steaks waited until last. After all, they believed they could settle the argument. "We are at the top of the food chain. We're the best. We're tops!"*

"Hey, wait a minute!" the plant on top of the refrigerator said. "I give off oxygen. I help the family breathe. What's more important than air?"*

"That's a good point," said the photos on the refrigerator door, "but there are things in life more important than food. Family is more important. We photos show the story of the family."*

"But what about me?" piped up the drawing made by the youngest child. "We pictures were placed here with much love. A little child drew me to say, 'I love you, Mom and Dad.' What's more important than showing love?"*

When the pictures said this, everything on top of the refrigerator and everything inside the refrigerator and everything on the outside of the refrigerator fell silent. Everything was thinking.

Then a tiny magnet cleared its throat. "Ahem. Excuse me." Its voice was hesitant and a little weak, but it grew in confidence as it made its point. "Food

and drink are important; they keep people alive. Plants are important because they help people breathe. Photos are important because family is important. And art pieces that children make are important because they show love. As you know, I'm just a little magnet. I don't feed people, and people never look upon me as a symbol of love. Actually, I'm overlooked. That's okay. I don't mind being second string. But aren't people drawn to the refrigerator door by the photos and artwork? I'm the one that draws people. They don't know that they're coming because of me. They think they're coming to the refrigerator for food or photos or art. I'm just a magnet, but I'm really good at drawing people together for food and fun and family."

No one spoke. Then the plant said, "I never really thought of you, Magnet. You *are* rather important."

The meat said, "Yeah, we just ham it up. Sometimes that's just a lot of bravado because deep down we're chicken."

The potatoes said, "Maybe all our bragging was too much. Thank you for knocking some of the starch out of us."

The carrots blushed, their orange skin turning a little red. "We help people's eyes, but we overlooked you."

The beverages felt a little sheepish, too. "We're so busy fizzing that we forget we're only a lot of bubbles without very much substance at all."

The photos said, "This is really a Kodak moment in our lives. Too bad we can't take a picture of what's going on inside us now. We're finally realizing that some of the best things in life are overlooked. I guess we miss the obvious."

Everyone began to shout, "Let's make the magnet king! Yes, King Magnet! Let the magnet reign over us!"

"No, no, no!" the magnet protested. "You're missing the point. No one is more important. We're all part of something bigger than ourselves. We're all needed in the Big Picture. We're all needed in God's plan. So let's just be ourselves—our best selves. And let's never argue about who is more important ever again."

"Yes, let's never argue again. Let's talk about really important things on Halloween. This is the night before people celebrate all the saints." And so from that Halloween on, when refrigerators come to life, everything on top of, inside, and on the refrigerators would talk about prayer and politics, family and friends, sunrises and sunsets.

So, remember the story of the magnet. It draws people to itself, but people never stop just to see the magnet. The magnet leads to photos or artwork. The magnet leads to food and drink. The magnet leads to family and friends. The magnet leads to love.

In the same way, each and every person is a magnet. Every person draws other people to himself or herself. But in friendship there is always something beyond. Ultimately the magnet leads the person to God.

Understanding the Story

1. Why did the meat and potatoes want to be important?

2. Do you have to be an important person to do what God wants you to do? Why or why not?

3. Why can small good deeds be important?

4. How can we lead other people to God like the magnet did?

5. How can a person be spectacular in the kingdom of God?

Suggested Activities

1. Encourage learners to collect items for their needy sisters and brothers in the Lord.

2. Ask a missionary to talk to the class about persons in a poor country.

3. Invite learners to share Halloween candy and treats with others, for example, by taking them to a soup kitchen.

4. Instead of trick-or-treating for candy, the children might collect money for a charity. Advise them to notify ahead of time, if possible, those whom they visit.

5. Have an All Saints Day party and ask learners to dress up like the saints.

6. Have everyone make paper pumpkins. Place inside large candles cut from bright yellow or gold paper as a reminder that they themselves will be saints if, like jack-o'-lanterns, they let God's light shine through them.

The Great Cranberry Revolt

Every day is a day to be thankful, but Thanksgiving is a time to be especially grateful. On Thanksgiving Day we thank God for blessings and we thank our families and friends for their goodness to us.

Do you know the gospel story about the ten lepers? Were they thankful? Today's story is "The Great Cranberry Revolt." Listen and find out how the cranberries felt when they were not appreciated, when no one noticed them.

The Scripture Reading

As Jesus entered a village, ten lepers approached him. Keeping their distance, they called out, saying, "Jesus, Master, have mercy on us!" When he saw them, he said to them, "Go and show yourselves to the priests." And as they went, they were made clean. Then one of them, when he saw that he was healed, turned back, praising God with a loud voice. He prostrated himself at Jesus' feet and thanked him. And he was a Samaritan. Then Jesus asked, "Were not ten made clean? But the other nine, where are they? Was none of them found to return and give praise to

God except this foreigner?" Then he said to him, "Get up and go on your way; your faith has made you well."
(Luke 17:12–19)

Understanding the Bible Story

1. What is a leper?
2. Why would the ten lepers say, "Jesus, Master, have mercy on us"?
3. Why did Jesus want to cure the lepers?
4. How many lepers returned?
5. How do you think Jesus felt when only one returned?
6. How can you thank God for blessings?

Meditation

Picture yourself in a place you like to be, whether it's a playground, the backyard, the beach, or your bedroom. You are enjoying yourself, perhaps playing a game. Jesus comes to play with you. Imagine yourself playing a game with Jesus. (*pause*) When you finish your game, you and Jesus talk together. You tell Jesus all the things you are grateful for, such as your parents, home, school, friends, favorite foods, pets, and so on. Spend some time thanking Jesus for all the good things you have. (*pause*) Thank him for all the good things he has given to your parish family: his life in the sacraments, the gospel, your care for one another. (*Pause in silence.*)

THE GREAT CRANBERRY REVOLT

In the middle of the story ask the children what they think the cranberries will do.

The Saturday before Thanksgiving Greg's Grocery was filled with shoppers buying turkey, potatoes, stuffing mix, pumpkin pie filling, and dinner rolls. The store's stockers could hardly keep the shelves and freezers full. The only Thanksgiving food that never needed to be replenished was the cranberry section.

Shoppers would check their list and notice that they hadn't put the cranberries in their cart. But instead of going down the aisle to get the berries or jelly, they shrugged their shoulders and said to themselves, "No one eats cranberries anyway. It's just part of the tradition. I think I'll just pass on the cranberries this year."

16

After the seventeenth shopper had snubbed the cranberries, Craig Cranberry got an idea. "I'm going to stop this nonsense of passing over us cranberries. We're all tired of being overlooked. Every year fewer and fewer people eat cranberries, and soon the tradition will disappear. People aren't mean; they just don't even notice us berries anymore. I need to call a meeting. I'll do it tonight when the grocery closes at 10:00."

That night Greg the Grocer emptied the cash registers, turned off the big lights, and locked the door behind him. He was exceptionally tired because the holiday business made his job that much harder. "Oh well," he sighed, "the profits will be good."

As soon as Craig Cranberry heard Greg's car start, he did not waste a second. He called out, "Hey, all you cranberries! You know why you're all still here? Because no one is buying us cranberries anymore! We need to do something about this, or the tradition of eating cranberries at Thanksgiving time will become extinct. Dinosaurs won't be the only ones caught in the bog. We will be, too."

"Well, what cran we do about it?" asked a package of berries named Coretta. ("Cran" is the way cranberries say "can.")

"What do you want us to do? Jump into every grocery cart when it passes by?" Corey, a can of jellied berries, remarked sarcastically.

Craig had thought he would get more cooperation than this. "We need to do something drastic, something that will draw attention, something to make headlines. I know! We'll revolt!"

"How are we going to do that?" Corey and Coretta exclaimed simultaneously.

"That's why I called this meeting. We've got to plan tonight and act tomorrow as soon as the store opens."

[Ask the children what they think the cranberries will do.]

The clock had just struck twelve when the meeting of the cranberries adjourned. They had their plan ready. Now they needed a few hours of sleep before the store opened at 8 AM.

Whistling, Greg the Grocer put his key into the lock and opened the door of the grocery store at 7:00. He flipped on the light switch, and the sudden glare made him blink. His whistling stopped in the middle of a note. He blinked once, then twice, then three times. Then he rubbed his eyes, thinking he might be only dreaming that he had come to the grocery store. After all, what he saw couldn't be real!

Little red berries were bouncing on every top shelf. Each one carried a sign: "Cranberries: America's native cultivated fruit." "We deserve a life beyond Thanksgiving." "Bacteria Blockers." "Holiday Jewels." "We give zing to muffins!"

Cans of jellied cranberries in groups of ten had formed pyramids in every

shopping cart. "We won't get out!" they chanted. "You must take us through the checkout." Cranberry cocktail juice bottles rolled down one aisle and up another like go-karts on a race track. "If you don't sip, you'll slip," they claimed, ready to pop their lids, making a Red Sea.

Realizing this was no nightmare, Greg the Grocer did something he would find very difficult to explain later: he talked to the cranberries. "What's going on here?" he demanded.

Craig, the ringleader, responded, "This is the Great Cranberry Revolt. We're tired of being the nice little red globs left on everybody's plate on Thanksgiving Day. We're tired of being thrown down garbage disposals by people who claim they cran't eat another bite but manage to down pumpkin pie. We're tired of being overlooked on your grocery shelves. Above all, we're fed up with being a tradition that is no longer traditional. We've got to put the cranberries back into Thanksgiving, and we know we cran."

"B-b-but the store will open in an hour! I can't have you all over the place. Now please go back to your freezers and shelves," Greg pleaded.

"Not so fast, Mr. Grocer. We're not going anywhere, and you cran't make us. Try to, and you're mincemeat pie." A dill pickle cannon loaded with whole cranberries moved into place. It was pointed at Greg's forehead. A volley of cranberries would cause a huge head-ache. Rigatoni noodle hoses filled with cranberry juice would stain everything they splashed. "No," Greg thought, "it won't pay to fight these red beasts. I'll just have to do as they say."

When the first customers entered the grocery store, they were welcomed by a can of cranberry sauce dangling from the rafters at eye level. The can of cranberry sauce was prepared with a smooth sales pitch. "Welcome to Cranberry Carnival! You never thought grocery shopping could be so much fun. Here's a cart complete with a pyramid of ten cans. Happy shopping!"

The pyramid of cans directed the shoppers' eyes to the top of the shelves. "Notice the bouncing cranberries. See how much energy they have. That same energy cran be yours. Just place two bags of whole cranberries in this shopping cart, then grind them for salad or use them in baking. You will be so full of vitamins. No wonder we cranberries are called the Incredible Edibles."

Then it was the bags' turn to give the final sales approach. "Just look at the beautiful color of the cranberry juice. Add this cocktail to soda and you'll have the perfect holiday punch. What is so pleasing to the eye is just as pleasing to the taste buds, so pick up two liters today." And, of course, the shoppers did.

That day every shopper left the store with ten cans of cranberry sauce, two packages of whole cranberries, and two liters of cranberry juice. And that Thanksgiving every household served cranberries first. The families and guests asked for second helpings of cranberries. That year the Great Cranberry Revolt saved cranberries from extinction.

Ever since, cranberries have grown in popularity. The cranberry float became the first in the Thanksgiving Macy's parade. Rudolph began using a cranberry for his red nose. Cranberry shrubs were added to evergreen wreaths. The cranberry became quite versatile. Cranberries even found a place in the American Hall of Fame, thanks to Craig the Cranberry's Great Cranberry Revolt.

Understanding the Story

1. Do you eat cranberries? Do you have cranberries at Thanksgiving?

2. Why did the cranberries revolt?

3. What did the cranberries do to get attention?

4. If you were a shopper, would you have bought cranberries?

5. Why did everyone start eating cranberries?

6. The point of the story is that everyone, even cranberries, needs thanks and appreciation. How do you thank your parents, grandparents, and siblings? How do you feel when you are thanked? How do you feel when no one thanks you?

Suggested Activities

1. As a class, use a sheet of poster board to make a list of things for which you are grateful.

2. Play a prayer-game by thanking God for things that begin with letters of the alphabet, in order; e.g., Thank you, God, for *apples*, *bicycles*, *cats*, *dogs*....

3. Play a prayer-game using crayons. Ask the children to close their eyes and select a crayon. They can take turns thanking God for things that are that color.

4. With your group decide which persons or organizations deserve your gratitude; for example, parents who provide their home, love, food, and care; administrators of the school or parish who provide learning and books to read; and so on. Together make Thanksgiving cards.

5. Invite learners to each make a turkey with many feathers. On each feather they can write something for which they are grateful.

6. The children might dramatize the ten lepers story, using their own words.

The Plastic
Soldier

CHRISTMAS
SEASON

RIGHT CHOICES

PEACE

Gather near a Christmas tree or manger scene.

Today we'll be listening to two stories about Christmas. The first story is from the Gospel of Luke. Luke tells us about the birth of Jesus in Bethlehem. Then we will hear the story of a plastic soldier who was lost and had to get back to his toy box. On his way he will learn an important lesson.

The Scripture Reading

Suggestion: Allow children to hold the figures from the crib, talk about each one, and hold them high whenever they are mentioned in the Lucan account.

In those days a decree went out from Emperor Augustus that all the world should be registered. All went to their own towns to be registered. Joseph also went from the town of Nazareth in Galilee to Judea, to the city of David called Bethlehem, because he was descended from the house and family of David. He went to be registered with Mary, to whom he was engaged and who was expecting a child. While they were there, the time came for her to deliver her child. And Mary gave birth to her firstborn son and wrapped him in bands of cloth, and laid him in a manger, because there was no place for them in the inn.

In that region there were shepherds living in the fields, keeping watch over their flock by night. Then an angel of the Lord stood before them, and the glory of the Lord shone around them, and they were terrified. But the angel said to them, "Do not be afraid; for see—I am bringing you good news of great joy for all the people: to you is born this day in the city of David a Savior, who is the Messiah, the Lord. This will be a sign for you: you will find a child wrapped in bands of cloth and lying in a manger." And suddenly there was with the angel a multitude of the heavenly host, praising God and saying, "Glory to God in the highest heaven, and on earth peace among those whom he favors!" When the angels had left them and gone into heaven, the shepherds said to one another, "Let us go now to Bethlehem and see this thing that has taken place, which the Lord has made known to us." So they went with haste and found Mary and Joseph, and the child lying in the manger. When they saw this, they made known what had been told them about this child; and all who heard it were amazed at what the shepherds told them. (Luke 2:1–18)

Understanding the Bible Story

1. Who are the parents of Jesus?

2. In what city was Jesus born?

3. Where was baby Jesus laid?

4. How did the shepherds learn about the birth of Jesus?

5. Why do you think the angel said, "Do not be afraid"?

6. What was the sign that the shepherds would see?

7. What did the shepherds see when they went to Bethlehem?

8. Why do you think the shepherds praised God?

Meditation

Imagine you are a shepherd. Hear the sheep saying, "Baa." Pretend you are looking up at the stars. Suddenly you see an angel! Do you feel a little afraid? Hear the angel sing "Glory to God!" (*pause*) Spend a few moments saying, "Glory to God!" in your heart. (*pause*) Hear the angel tell you to go to Bethlehem to see the child lying in the manger. (*pause*) In your imagination gather your sheep. Off you go! (*pause*) When you arrive at the stable, you greet Mary and Joseph. (*pause*) Ask to hold the baby's hand. Now talk to Jesus, the Prince of Peace. Tell Jesus whatever you want. Maybe ask Jesus to make you more peace-filled and to help you avoid fighting and quarreling. Ask Jesus to bless your family's Christmas season. Thank Jesus for coming to earth to be with us. (*Pause in silence.*)

THE PLASTIC SOLDIER

"Aaron, pick up your toys. It's time to go to karate lessons," Mom called. Normally Aaron would have to be called at least twice, but this day he scooped up his army men, as well as their camouflage bushes and trees, and dropped them into the toy box.

In his hurry, Aaron left one plastic soldier under the sofa, the soldier's head peeking out the ruffled upholstery. The plastic soldier looked all around. His comrades had deserted him. Where was everyone?

Something moved, and the plastic soldier raised his rifle, ready to protect himself. Big, wondering eyes looked down at the plastic soldier. Then a mouth opened showing pointed teeth. It was the family cat. Because it was bigger than the plastic soldier, the family cat looked like a lion. Expecting a huge roar, the plastic soldier heard only "Meow. Meow." Fortunately for the plastic soldier, the cat could not smell this new object under the sofa.

She soon lost interest in the plastic soldier. The cat turned away to find something more interesting, like catnip or a warm spot for another cat nap. Then the plastic soldier called out, "Hey, cat! Get me out of here! I want to get back to my buddies!" **[Hey, cat! Get me out of here! I want to get back to my buddies!]**

The cat turned around, sniffed the plastic soldier once more, and almost walked away again. The plastic soldier repeated: "Please, cat! Get me out of here! I belong in the box with the other soldiers. I don't want to lose my troop."

"What can I do to help?" **[What can I do to help?]** the cat asked.

"Couldn't I ride on your back? That would be so much faster. I'd be sitting up higher than if I were just walking on the floor. I'd be able to find that toy box and my troop," the plastic soldier explained.

The cat bent down, and the plastic soldier grabbed her fur. He pulled himself up and rode bareback. From his seat on the cat, the plastic soldier felt he was king of the world. This was so much better than letting Aaron deploy him and the other soldiers for fake battles!

"Giddy-up!" **[Giddy-up!]** yelled the plastic soldier, and the cat moved more swiftly. "Whoa!" **[Whoa!]** the plastic

23

soldier called out, and the cat came to a dead stop on all four paws. "To the left! Now to the right!" **[To the left! Now to the right!]** Whatever the soldier said, the cat obeyed. "This is such fun!" the soldier thought. "I could order everyone around. Hey, I've got a great idea! I'll declare myself a general. General Plastic. That's my name. Now, let's see what I can do with my new title. I know. I'll ride around on my horse that's really a cat. I'll tell everyone and everything in sight to obey me."

"Cat, from now on you're going to be my horse," **[Cat, from now on you're going to be my horse.]** declared General Plastic.

Cat was more than a little surprised, but she decided to humor the plastic soldier. "Okay, I'll be your horse, but you can't wear spurs. Where do you want to go?" **[Where do you want to go?]**

"Let's invade the kitchen. **[Let's invade the kitchen.]** I can take over the whole territory, and all that food will be mine," said General Plastic.

"Meow…er, I mean…Gr-r-r-owl…er, I mean, Neigh!" **[Neigh!]** roared and whinnied the cat. She was quite uncertain what a military cat-horse should call out in battle cry.

General Plastic reined in his cat-horse in the doorway of the kitchen. "I

need to plan my tactics. First, I'll crawl under the sink to loosen the pipe. That will form a huge river, flooding out half the enemy. Giddy-up!"

Off they went across the kitchen floor and stopped before the cupboard, below the sink. The general used all his might to open the doors. He crawled in and swung himself up on the pipe. Grasping the piece between the two pipes, the general used his whole body to turn it. After several minutes the connection budged. Soon water gushed onto the kitchen floor. "I'm a great general," the plastic soldier thought. He knew he could cause even more destruction.

Forgetting cats don't like water, General Plastic urged his cat-horse to go to the wastebasket. Reluctantly the cat tiptoed through the river in a place where her paws barely got wet. "I'll build barriers that my enemies can't cross," said the general, as he toppled a wastebasket.

"We have to reconnoiter. I need to get to the top of that hill—I mean, cupboard."

"Wait just a minute," **[Wait just a minute.]** complained the cat-horse. "Just how do you expect me to get up there?"

"Easy," said the general. "Just jump up on the chair, then leap up to the table. Then take a leap over to the counter. I'll manage from there to get to the cupboard."

"This is cool!" **[This is cool!]** thought the cat. Her master never let her climb up on the table. She had always want-

ed to do it. She didn't stop to think that she could get into trouble. After all, this was war!

Cat-horse surprised herself at how quickly she could get the general to the countertop. The general grabbed a telephone cord and climbed his way to the cupboard. What a view! He could look over the whole kitchen and part of the living room. But there was no toy box in sight. Oh well, he didn't need the other soldiers. He was doing quite well as a one-man army, giving his own orders and obeying his own orders. "While I'm up here, I might as well drop some bombs." With that, he got behind a peanut butter jar and pushed. "Bombs away!" **[Bombs away!]** He looked over the ledge to see where the bomb had dropped. It made a huge noise, but it didn't really cause any destruction. "I must find more destructive bombs." General Plastic thought nothing could be more damaging than ketchup bottles, pickle jars, and maple syrup. Down they all went. Crash! Red, green, and brown gook spread over the wet floor. They formed thin islands in the river.

"Hey!" yelled the cat. "You're really making a mess. **[You're really making a mess.]** The family may think I did all this. No more!"

The general agreed and thanked the cat-horse for all her help. He swung back down the phone cord and leaped from the counter to the table. He then slid down a table leg to the floor. The family room was next. Perhaps he'd find the toy box and the other military men there. As he searched for the toy box, the general was surprised to see a cow barn in front of him. What was a cow stall doing in the family room? General Plastic remembered that things were much smaller than they seemed. Perhaps this was a toy cow barn, something like a playhouse. He could imagine a child playing with a playhouse, but whatever would a child play with a cow barn? He marched up to the cow barn and nearly stumbled over a sheep lying in the imitation straw.

"Don't hurt yourself."

"Who said that?" wondered General Plastic. Peering inside the cow barn the general noticed a man and a woman. The woman was holding a newborn baby. The man was lining the cow's trough with fresh straw. The man looked at him kindly and said, "Come on in. We were just going to make a little supper. Just a hot drink and some bread. Would you like to stay?"

General Plastic thought the couple and their baby were rather unusual. He didn't know anyone else lived here except the boy and his parents. Somewhat tongue-tied the general hesitated until he saw the man make a place to sit down in the clean straw. "All right. Thank you." Once seated he said, "I'm General Plastic. I'm looking for my buddies. I'm separated from the rest of my troop. I can't fight a war without them."

"Welcome. My name is Joseph, and this is my wife, Mary. We are the proud parents of Jesus." Joseph gave Mary a hug, then lifted the blanket from the face of Jesus. A beautiful baby boy lay sleeping.

"So you say you fight wars?" Joseph began the conversation. "I've always wondered why people fight a war."

"Well, you fight wars to gain more land. And you fight wars to feel powerful. When you fight wars, you know who is better," explained the general.

Joseph shook his head. He didn't understand the sense of war. "Our newborn baby is the Prince of Peace. He came to this world from heaven, so no one will fight wars. He came to bring peace to everyone, even you."

General Plastic looked down at the sleeping baby. "Is this baby really a prince? The Prince of Peace?" **[The Prince of Peace?]**

"Yes," said Joseph and Mary.

General Plastic knew that his own power was not much at all next to the power of a prince. Why, this baby was more powerful than a commanding officer! General Plastic quickly stood at attention and saluted. The baby yawned and opened his eyes. General Plastic knew that he would never be able to fight again. He had seen the Prince of Peace face to face.

"Well, I have to find my buddies. Thank you for your welcome. And thanks for making me think differently about war." General Plastic saluted and walked outside the cow barn.

Suddenly General Plastic was lifted high into the air. The boy, Aaron, had just returned from his karate lessons. "How did you get way over here?"

Aaron said to the plastic general. He plunked the soldier down in the toy box with the other military men. General Plastic was glad to be back with his men.

"Guys, I met the Prince of Peace. There never has to be another war. Can you believe it?" General Plastic called out to his comrades. "It's true! Let me tell you about it. **[Let me tell you about it.]** Well, first, I had to get myself a horse...."

■ ■ ■

Understanding the Story

1. Where did the plastic soldier want to go?

2. What made the plastic soldier feel like a king?

3. Did the plastic soldier change after he felt like a king?

4. Joseph did not understand the point of war. How did the plastic soldier explain war's purpose?

5. Jesus has many special titles. What was the title Joseph used?

6. Why couldn't the plastic soldier fight anymore?

7. Sometimes you have some power; for example, you can do something that no one else in your family or group can. When you have power, how should you use it? Can power help you do good things?

8. How do you get power? Can you be powerful if you are not a king or a military leader?

9. Sometimes Jesus seemed weak. He seemed to have no power when he was lying in the manger or when he died on the cross. But he still had power. Why didn't Jesus use his power?

10. As followers of Jesus, we should be peacemakers. How can you be a peacemaker in your family? with your classmates? in your school or religious education program?

Suggested Activities

1. Encourage your learners: Be a peacemaker at home. Obey your parents and grandparents and caregivers. Be nice to your brothers and sisters. Do not fight or argue.

2. Have the children draw their own manger scenes and put themselves in it. They can show the picture of the birthday gift they are giving Jesus.

3. Ask your learners to think about how they and their family can give a Christmas gift to someone in need.

4. Invite the children to write a news article about someone they know or have read about who did a good deed for another person or group.

Robert Robot

BAPTISM OF
OUR LORD

VOCATION
AWARENESS

LISTENING TO
GOD

PRAYER

When Jesus was on earth, he listened to his Father. He tried to hear what his Father wanted him to do. When Jesus was baptized, he heard his Father say from heaven, "You are my Son, the Beloved; with you I am well pleased" (Mark 1:11). God speaks to us. We need to listen for the voice of God who speaks to our hearts and in many other ways.

The Scripture Reading

In those days Jesus came from Nazareth of Galilee and was baptized by John in the Jordan. And just as he was coming up out of the water, he saw the heavens torn apart and the Spirit descending like a dove on him. And a voice came from heaven, "You are my Son, the Beloved; with you I am well pleased."

And the Spirit immediately drove him out into the wilderness. He was in the wilderness forty days, tempted by Satan; and he was with the wild beasts; and the angels waited on him. (Mark 1:9–13)

Understanding the Bible Story

1. Where was Jesus baptized? Who baptized him?
2. What did Jesus see when he came out of the water?
3. What did Jesus hear when he came out of the water?
4. Why did Jesus go into the desert?
5. How long did Jesus stay in the desert?

Meditation

Imagine that you are in your backyard at night. You have a tent for you and a friend. You are looking at the stars, but your friend falls asleep. (*pause*) As you continue looking at the stars, you hear God say to you, "Hi! Are you having fun camping outside? I'd like to talk with you for a while. I have a few things to say." Spend a few minutes listening to what God says to you. (*Pause in silence.*)

ROBERT ROBOT

At each asterisk (*) the children can make sounds and/ or motions, such as cupping their ears, to depict a robot that's listening.

The year was 3025 AD. Humans had lived on Mars from 2528 to 3001 AD. Now all the humans had died, and only their robots remained. There were 800 robots that roamed the red planet doing what they had been programmed to do. After a thousand years they would need to be recharged. Some scanned the atmosphere for foreign objects that might invade Mars. Others kept track of weather patterns. Still others sent signals to Planet Earth. The robots beeped along doing their assigned task, except for one little robot named Robert.

Robert had come to life—that is, been invented—by the last scientist alive on Mars. Robert had not had a chance to be programmed, so he did not know what he was meant to do. Who ever heard of a robot that wasn't programmed? The other 799 robots called him "Loser." They never wanted to be seen near him. This made Robert very sad and lonely. But that wasn't all. On each side of his head Robert had round metal pieces that looked like melons cut in half. No other robot had them. To the others Robert looked like a freak or a monster. Not only did the robots stay away from him, some even

ran when they saw him. "A monster!" they screamed. Poor Robert!

Robert did not beep to Planet Earth, so no sounds came from him. He had no camera, so he took no pictures. He had no drills to dig deep holes so he could find hidden water from lakes of long ago. He had no traction to go into craters. All he had was an ugly metal piece on each side of his head. Robert could not even look at his reflection on the silver backs of other robots. He thought he was too ugly. Would Robert be miserable for another 976 years?

One Mars day Robert was looking out into space when he saw a brilliant beam of light. Was it a shooting star? Was this the approach of some new galaxy? Did planets align themselves? Did something explode? As he watched, the beam of light drew near. It got bigger and bigger and bigger, and it took on the force of a tornado. The light swirled around him, and he felt caught in a whirlwind. Would he be sucked up and whisked off the planet? Fright seized him.

Then just as suddenly he knew he should not be afraid. How did he know that? He heard, "Do not be afraid." How could he receive such a signal when he was not programmed to receive any?

In just a few seconds the force of the whirlwind lessened. It seemed to be drawing away. Before it left, the light that was like a tornado tapped each metal piece on the sides of Robert's head seven times. Then it was gone.

Robert sat amazed. What was it? What did it mean? Did any of the other robots see the light and feel the tornado? And what did the tapping on the sides of his head mean?

Without really understanding what he was doing, Robert began to listen.* He kept hearing, "Do not be afraid." The words were so pleasant, so soft, so soothing. Could the light that was like a tornado have been a creature of some sort? Perhaps it was from outside the universe.

"Yes, Robert, I'm from God," Robert heard. Where had the voice come from? The metal pieces on the sides of his head vibrated. Suddenly Robert realized he could listen through them. He strained to hear and he picked up more signals.* They were not like the signals that the other robots heard. They were not like the signals that the other robots sent. These were signals without words or beeps. Could there be such a thing as wordless words and beepless beeps?

Then Robert heard another message: "Listen to me. I am the God who made the universe. I am the Master of all the humans who created you robots. I am the Creator of everything!" With that Robert began to shake. He was terrified, but then he heard the wordless words again, "Be not afraid."

What was this wonderful thing? Robert would try it himself. Without words or beeps Robert communicated, "God, what do you want of me?" Then his head pieces vibrated again.* In came more wordless words and beepless beeps: "Listen to me. I will guide you. You are to tell the other robots about who I am."

"Okay, God," Robert said. His head pieces stopped vibrating. He sat there for a long time waiting for another message. None came.

A group of robots came ambling by. "There's ugly Robert!" one called.

Robert ignored the remark. Instead he said to the robots, "I have good news. God has spoken to us robots on Mars." The robots laughed. They didn't believe him. But Robert just kept telling every robot he met, "I have good news. God has spoken to us robots on Mars." Some began to believe Robert. They asked how they could hear God.

Robert said, "From now on I am going to call these pieces on my head my God radar. You have to wear God radar like mine." The other robots knew they would be laughed at if they looked as silly as Robert, but they really, really, really wanted to hear God. So they began to put on God radar. They too heard the voice of God without words or beeps.*

This small group of robots met once a week at night to share their messages. Sometimes one would hear, "I love you." Another would hear, "Follow me." Another would know that he should be kind and forgiving, even if he was called ugly. They always spent part of their time together just sitting quietly and listening.*

Eventually the little band of robots was called "The Listeners." Every year more robots joined their group. Together they agreed on a Mars Mission. They signed an agreement that said, "We, the Listeners, will be alert to God. We will try to help all other robots hear God's voice."*

The band of listeners wanted to make Robert their leader, but Robert listened to God.* God said, "You are all my followers. I am your Leader." So the band just kept listening and lived as one.* They are still living to this day and have at least 864 more years of listening ahead of them before their charge wears out.

Robert Robot is still hearing messages. He is sending a message to you. Can you hear it?* The message is this, "Listen to God. God loves you."

■ ■ ■

Understanding the Story

1. Why didn't the other robots like Robert?

2. What did the light that was like a tornado tell Robert?

3. What was different about the messages Robert received?

4. Who was speaking without words to Robert?

5. Why do you think other robots joined Robert?

6. Can you hear God tell you "I love you"?

Suggested Activities

1. Invite a religious sister or brother, a deacon, or a priest to speak to the children about his or her vocation.

2. As a class, make a card for someone who is becoming a priest or sister. Thank the person for following the call of God.

3. Invite your learners to draw a picture of Robert Robot or of themselves listening to God. Or they can write a continuation of the story.

4. Write the word "listen" vertically on the board. Ask the learners to think of words that begin with each of those letters, words that remind the children how they are to listen to God; for example, with *love*.

5. Suggest to learners: Decide with your family on a time when you all can spend time listening to and praying to God, for example, before a meal or in the evening.

Praise Bugs

VALENTINE'S
DAY

PRAISE

CARE FOR
OTHERS

Valentine's Day is a day on which we express our love for others by sending valentines or giving candy and flowers. Because God is Love, Valentine's Day is a day on which to show our love for God and experience God's love for us. Think about how God shows love in the Bible story. Then think about how you can praise God when you hear the second story, "Praise Bugs."

The Scripture Reading

In those days when there was again a great crowd without anything to eat, Jesus called his disciples and said to them, "I have compassion for the crowd, because they have been with me now for three days and have nothing to eat. If I send them away hungry to their homes, they will faint on the way—and some of them have come from a great distance." His disciples replied, "How can one feed these people with bread here in the desert?" He asked them, "How many loaves do you have?" They said, "Seven." Then he ordered the crowd to sit down on the ground; and he took the seven loaves, and after giving thanks he broke them and gave them to his disciples to distribute; and they distributed them to the crowd. They had also a few small fish; and after blessing them, he ordered that these too should be distributed. They ate and were filled; and they took up the broken pieces left over, seven baskets full. Now there were about four thousand people. And he sent them away. (Mark 8:1–9)

Understanding the Bible Story

1. Why did Jesus decide to feed the crowd?

2. How many loaves of bread did Jesus have?

3. What did Jesus do with the seven loaves of bread?

4. How many people were fed? Was there enough to eat?

Meditation

Pretend that you are in the crowd listening to Jesus. You are getting hungry, so you feel glad when Jesus asks, "How many loaves do you have?" Your family has a loaf, so you make a contribution. Soon there are six more loaves. Jesus takes the seven loaves, blesses them, and everyone gets something to eat. (*pause*) Later you are picking up the leftovers with other children and teens. When you take the leftovers to Jesus, you have a chance to speak to him. What would you like to tell Jesus? Tell him now. (*Pause in silence.*)

PRAISE BUGS

Before reading the story, instruct the children to flap their arms like wings whenever they hear the word "buzz."

Beulah Bug had been the head of the Parish School of Religion program for as long as anyone could remember. Every time a first-grade bug enrolled in the program, Beulah would say, "I taught your father" or "I taught your mother" or "I taught your grandmother" or "I taught your great-uncle." Even though she was getting up in years, she knew all the recent "buzz" words. "Buzz, buzz, buzz" she would say, before she went on with the rest of her sentence.

Every year on Saint Valentine's Day, Beulah Bug would create a contest. She had been doing this for forty-seven years, but she never repeated an idea. She would have Bible Bumble Bees, New Testament Olympics, Psalm

Recitals, Proverbs Programs, Gospel Galas, and much more—relays, races, songfests, and contests of making hearts by tearing paper behind one's back. Each year she sponsored something original. This year, though, she was perplexed. What could she do that she had never done before? As she sat there thinking, the doorbell rang. It was an old friend, Alice Aphid.

"Buzz, buzz, buzz. Well, praise the Lord!" Beulah exclaimed at the sight of Alice.

"Yes, praise the Lord indeed!" Alice exclaimed.

Instantly Beulah had her contest idea. She would have a contest of poems to praise God. "Buzz, buzz, buzz. Alice, you just gave me an idea!"

"How could I have done that? I just got here."

"Buzz, buzz, buzz. When we praised the Lord, I knew what I would do for this year's contest. Let's have the children write poems of praise. What do you think?"

Well, Alice was an aphid who had a thought for everything, so she and Beulah sat right down to make the rules for the contest. As they sipped nectar from teacups, they wrote the rules.

"The poem cannot be too long. These are children. Don't you think four lines would be nice?" asked Alice.

"Buzz, buzz, buzz. Why, yes," said Beulah, "quatrains are very nice." (She was proud that she remembered the big word that meant a poem of four lines.) "And they should rhyme, too. Kids love to make rhymes."

"Yes, and it's for Valentine's Day, so the children should put their poem inside a heart, don't you think?" asked Alice.

They flew over to the computer, chose a font and border, and began making advertisements for all the classrooms. Each sign said, "Praise Bugs Contest. All entries must be four lines that include at least one rhyme. In honor of Valentine's Day write your entry on heart-shaped paper. Entries must be postmarked no later than February 7. Winners will be announced on February 14. All participants will receive a red t-shirt saying 'Bugs praise the Lord!' The top prizes will be $100, $50, and $25."

The next Sunday all the teachers in Beulah Bug's Parish School of Religion gave the bug children the advertisement and encouraged them to write poems that praise God.

That afternoon many households spent time as a family thinking up rhyming words and ideas to praise God. Stores received phone calls to see whether they sold rhyming dictionaries. Parents helped their sons and daughters look through psalms to get ideas. Dads gave up their Sunday afternoon naps to run to the store for red paper. Moms wrote out the alphabet and sound blends so their children could experiment: say, sway, stray, spray, stay.

The Ladybug Family sat around the dinner table after the dishes were cleared. Mom, Dad, Lydia, Larry, and Lenore thought they created a winner. They wrote

Violets are violet,
roses are red,
praise the Lord of Life
that we're not dead.

They thought this was a great poem because so often people killed bugs. They wanted to thank God that their family was still together.

The Caterpillars in their condominium decided to go to the neighborhood pool. As they swam, Cathy, Carl, and Caitlyn made up lines to the ideas their parents called out to them from the recliners on the edge of the pool. After two games of keep-away and three races across the length of the pool, the Caterpillar family came up with this poem:

Caterpillars are great.
Caterpillars can transform.
We will become butterflies.
Praise God we won't stay worms.

The Caterpillars thought they'd win, because all Christians need to transform their lives.

The Centipedes sat in their family room around the big table on which they played games. The table was covered with dictionaries and thesauruses, notebook paper and pencils. The recycle basket was overflowing with many failed attempts. Finally they thought they had the poem that was a shoe-in for the contest. (Centipedes like to boast that they have a hundred legs, so they felt their chances were 100 to 1 that they'd get top prize. It

was like a hundred shoe-ins!) This is what they wrote:

Centipedes are quick,
yes, they're very fast.
Praise God, for God's
forgiveness will always last.

The Adler Ant family worked industriously. They knew they could carry big words, bigger than themselves, so they tackled God's praises with a prodigious vocabulary. They wrote

Jesus endured the cross,
expiating our sins.
He told us to pick up our crosses
if disciples we'll be.
Our baptism and confirmation
have made us witnesses
His death and rising
we attest courageously.

Meanwhile the Moth Family fasted from wool for three days to ask God's blessing upon their writing. When they set pen to paper, this is the quatrain they wrote:

Praise God for six days of creation.
God made land, sea, sky,
birds, bugs, and trees.
Praise God for sharing his creativity.
Praise God with your voices
and on your knees.

February 7 finally arrived. Beulah and Alice checked their mailbox one more time before they began reading the entries.

"Buzz, buzz, buzz. There are so many poems. It will take us days to read them all," declared Beulah.

"But look at the good side. We'll be praising God the whole time we make our decision," noted Alice.

Alice and Beulah sipped nectar while they read all the praises of God. They brewed pot after pot, and the stacks of poems piled up higher and higher. The good poems were placed in a basket with a sign saying, "Possible winners." The stack measured two feet. The other basket labeled "Rejects" did not have a single poem.

Would they have to read all of them again to find the winners?

Once again Alice came to the rescue. "Why don't we say that everyone is a winner?"

"Buzz, buzz, buzz. What about the money prizes?" responded Beulah.

"We'll put the money together and use the $175 to throw a big Valentine's party for all the families who submitted a poem."

"Buzz, buzz, buzz. That's a great idea! We could have a Praise Jamboree, too!"

The next Sunday Beulah Bug announced that everyone was a winner. Everyone was invited to an ice cream social, complete with Valentine's Day decorations.

That evening all the bugs hopped, crawled, or flew to the big tent on the parish property.

They enjoyed chocolate fudge sundaes, pineapple topping over vanilla, pecans over peppermint, strawberries over strawberry ice cream, sprinkles over bubblegum ice cream, and whipped cream over pistachio.

After everyone had eaten, they spent the whole night under the full moon crooning their lyrics of praise to the God who created them. As the sun rose over the hill and the moon faded into the morning clouds, they sang one last song to their Creator. Its melody was "Twinkle, Twinkle Little Star." You can sing it, too.

Praise Bugs, Praise Bugs love to sing,
"God is great. Our God is king."
Give God glory every day.
Make God first in every way.
Praise Bugs, Praise Bugs—
that's our name.
Let your prayer be just the same.

Understanding the Story

1. Was it a good idea to have a party instead of giving three cash prizes?

2. Which poem of praise did you like the best?

3. When we praise someone, how do we do it? When we praise God, how can we do it?

4. Why should we praise God?

5. Can you make up a praise prayer to Jesus for feeding the crowd?

6. Jesus gave bread to those in need. Saint Valentine gave money to those who were poor. How can we be like Jesus and Saint Valentine? What can we give to the needy?

Suggested Activities

1. Invite the children to make a valentine for Jesus, expressing their love for him.

2. Frost valentine cookies and take them to a residence for elders.

3. Together dramatize the story "Praise Bugs." Enact it for an audience, such as children of another grade level or residents in assisted living.

4. Memorize the song "Praise Bugs Love to Sing."

5. As a class make a mural of the story with crayon or paint. Or use modeling clay to make the various bugs. Tell the story again using the children's creations.

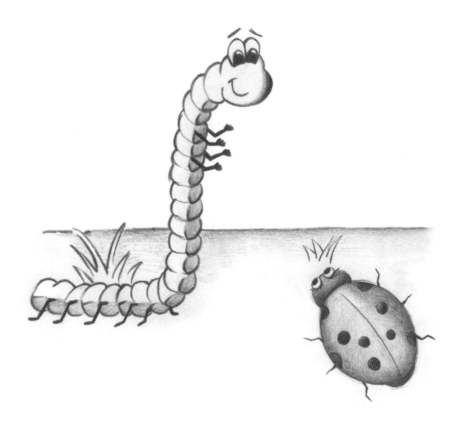

The King Who Favored Orange

On patriotic holidays we honor leaders in our country, such as President George Washington and Martin Luther King, Jr. Good leaders do what is best for their followers.

In today's two stories we will see Jesus as a good leader and king. You will also hear about a little king who was a bad leader. As you listen, try to figure out what makes a good leader.

The Scripture Reading

Then Pilate entered the headquarters again, summoned Jesus, and asked him, "Are you the King of the Jews?" Jesus answered, "Do you ask this on your own, or did others tell you about me?" Pilate replied, "I am not a Jew, am I? Your own nation and the chief priests have handed you over to me. What have you done?" Jesus answered, "My kingdom is not from this world. If my kingdom were from this world, my followers would be fighting to keep me from being handed over to the Jews. But as it is, my kingdom is not from here."
(John 18:33–36)

Understanding the Bible Story

1. Who was Pilate? Why was he talking to Jesus?

2. Where is the kingdom of Jesus?

3. If Jesus is the king, who are the people in his kingdom?

4. What would happen to Jesus soon after this meeting with Pilate?

5. Is Jesus like the kings you read about in fairy tales and see in cartoons?

6. Jesus had almighty power. Did he show almighty power when he was on earth? When could Jesus have used his power to help himself, but didn't?

Meditation

Imagine that this is the day Jesus will be put on the cross. You are in the crowd when people yell, "Crucify him!" You are surprised and angry that anyone would want to put Jesus to death. You try to yell above the noise, "No, please don't kill him! He doesn't deserve to die! Jesus is a good man!" But no one hears you. (*pause*) As Jesus carries his cross, you meet him along the way to Calvary. You have a few seconds to talk with Jesus before a guard pushes you away. What would you say to Jesus? Tell him now. (*Pause in silence.*)

THE KING WHO FAVORED ORANGE

During the reading of the story, have the children perform a simple action such as waving or standing up or clapping their hands whenever the word "orange" is read.

Once upon a time a new king was born. Unfortunately he became spoiled very quickly, learning to demand whatever he wanted at the moment. His every whim was satisfied immediately. "I don't want oatmeal!" he'd scream. "Give me chocolate pudding!"

Of course, because he was king, everyone would hurry to do his bidding. Unfortunately he never spoke softly, nor were his wishes easy to fulfill. Day in and day out the servants in the kingdom scurried around, meeting the little king's every wish. The only good result of the king's screaming was a new manufacturing company for earplugs. To prevent everyone in

the kingdom from going deaf, Earplug Enterprise had a wonderful array of objects to block out the king's shouts. Of course, people could only use them when they weren't on duty. The most fashionable female servants wore colorful scarves over their ears. The most technological servants wore little receptors over their ears that changed sound waves into light waves. They would aim the light waves wherever they needed light, and their electrical bills dropped considerably.

On one very humid day the little king should have gotten up on the other side of the bed instead of making everyone put up with his bad mood. He gave the following order: "Everything in my kingdom shall be colored orange. Orange is my favorite color."

Well, all those who had a half-day off removed their earplugs to know whether they had heard correctly. Those without earplugs were completely bowled over by the news—to say nothing of its volume. The head servants looked at the lower servants. For once the lower servants were glad they were lower servants. They would not have to figure out how to carry out this command.

The head servants had a meeting to decide what could be done to make everything orange. They argued, they wrangled, they beat their heads against the walls of the castle, but they could not come up with a plan. "This will simply never do. An orange kingdom indeed!" So they decided that Howard

would tell the king that the demand was absolutely impossible. Would the king mind reconsidering?

Now Howard happened to be a coward. Who wouldn't be in such circumstances? So he practiced what he would say. "King, my dear little king, it is impossible to kake your mingdom orange." No, that would never do—mixing up his consonants. "Your Excellency...cy...cy...cy, p-p-p-p-p-p-please note how drab the k-k-k-k-k-k-k-kingdom will be if it had no b-b-b-b-b-b-blue, g-g-g-g-g-g-g-green, y-y-y-y-y-yellow, b-b-b-b-b-b-brown, or p-p-p-p-p-p-p-purple." Howard would never be able to say this sentence because he stuttered too much. Besides, the king had made a decree the month before that whenever anyone recited colors, he had to say all the colors contained in a box of ninety-six crayons. It would take all day for Howard to name the crayons if he stuttered.

Instead, Howard decided to e-mail the king. This is what he typed: "Your Excellency, the color orange is a most exquisite color. Orange is the perfect compliment to your blue eyes.

"Orange is the color most seen along the kingdom's highways during the summer. Orange smells like citrus fruit, and it tastes good just to look at it. But please understand that your kingdom will be destroyed if everything is made orange. The moat will look like orange juice. The trees will look like lollipops. The insects that are attracted by different colors will never find the right flowers to pollinate. All the vegetation will die. People will starve because animals will not eat orange grass. Restaurants will lose business because who would eat orange steaks? Please reconsider, O King. Let your favor rest on all colors as they now are."

Because the king was too young to read, his Chief E-mail Reader read aloud to the king all his e-mails. When the Chief E-mail Reader saw this message, he knew the king would be so angry that he would have the Reader killed on the spot. He had to do some quick thinking. Fortunately the Chief E-mail Reader was also one of the kingdom's artists-in-residence.

"O King, an important e-mail came today. It praises you on your excellent choice of orange for everything in your kingdom. But in order to fully appreciate orange, could we, the artists of the realm, make a few sugges-

tions? To fully highlight the beauty of orange, could the grass be kept green? And what about keeping the sky blue? Maybe rocks and tree trunks could be black. Flowers might be multicolored. In this way orange would be made even more beautiful by reason of its contrast with the other colors."

The king was not used to receiving suggestions, but to the surprise of everyone he agreed.

The young king issued the following decree: "From henceforth the sky will be blue, the grass will be green, the rocks and tree trunks will be black, and flowers will be multicolored." The king never realized that nothing had changed. Everything in the kingdom stayed exactly as it was meant to be. But nobody breathed a word, and the king continued to think he had made his whole kingdom orange, because that's the color he favored.

Understanding the Story

1. Would you have liked to be part of the little king's kingdom?

2. Was it a good idea to make everything orange?

3. Why was it a good idea to keep the grass green and the sky blue?

4. What do you think about the way the king used his power?

5. In what ways were Jesus and the little king different? Who made the better king?

Suggested Activities

1. Discuss ways to be a good leader at home and in school.

2. Ask your learners to draw a picture of or write about someone who has power and uses it to help people.

3. Use construction paper and other materials to fashion jewels or other gifts to give to Jesus, our king. What will they give? Why?

4. Have the children act out a situation in which Jesus uses his power to do something good.

5. Discuss one practical thing your learners can do to make a positive change at school or in the neighborhood.

St. Patrick's Day Treasure

ST. PATRICK'S
DAY

REAL
TREASURE

COOPERATION

Jesus told parables, stories that have a hidden meaning. We have to look hard to see what the story means. Seeds may be God's words. Pearls may be God's kingdom. Today we will hear a story about treasure.

The Scripture Reading

Jesus said, "The kingdom of heaven is like treasure hidden in a field, which someone found and hid; then in his joy he goes and sells all that he has and buys that field.

Again, the kingdom of heaven is like a merchant in search of fine pearls; on finding one pearl of great value, he went and sold all that he had and bought it." (Matthew 13:44–46)

Understanding the Bible Story

1. What did the man find in the field?

2. Why did the man want to buy the field?

3. Besides the field, what else would the man get when he bought the field?

4. What was the treasure?

5. What was Jesus teaching us with these parables?

Meditation

Pretend Jesus has given you a treasure map and begin to read it now along with me. See yourself as a little baby. Thank Jesus for being born. (*pause*) See the font in which you were baptized. Thank Jesus for the gift of eternal life begun at baptism. (*pause*) Pretend that your family and friends are all gathered round you, and they are celebrating your birthday. Tell Jesus how much you treasure your family and friends. (*pause*) See yourself at Sunday Mass. Tell Jesus that you treasure this part of the week when you can pray to him with the community. (*pause*) Imagine yourself doing all the things Jesus would: he obeyed his parents, he played games fairly, he tried hard in school, and he grew up doing what God his Father wanted. Ask Jesus to make you more like him. (*pause*) Someday you will be with Jesus in heaven. Heaven is the best treasure of all. Tell Jesus that you want to be with him in heaven some day. (*Pause in silence.*)

ST. PATRICK'S DAY TREASURE

Tell the children that whenever they hear the word "green," they are to stand. Perhaps you can give each of them a piece of green candy at the end.

Patrick McCabe was born on St. Patrick's Day. How is that for Irish luck? Patrick thought he was the luckiest boy in the world. This year on St. Patrick's Day he was going to have a party.

Green balloons marked the house, leprechaun place favors dotted the tables, and shamrocks hung from the doorways and ceiling. Soon the guests arrived, and the games began. Boys from his school and Scout troop guessed the number of green jellybeans in a jar, threw coins into pots of gold, and put their heads together over a game of Irish proverbs. But the best activity was still to come.

Above the noise, Patrick's dad called to the boys, "Hey, boys, how about a treasure hunt?" Shouts of delight filled the room. "Well, we have to get you organized in teams. Let's count off." Having determined the two teams of six, Patrick's father handed the captain of each team a treasure map.

Burnt at the edges and tied with a raggedy green ribbon, the maps looked very old and real.

While one team ran outside, the other team rolled out their map on the living room floor. At first they were quite puzzled until familiar objects began to appear. "Here's where we start—the garage," said Sam. "And that's the stop sign on the corner," Bill added. "That's the water tower!" Phil exclaimed. "I bet that green shape is the ball diamond," Patrick said with confidence. It was time to get outside, and the boys raced to the garage. On their way they saw the other team turning the corner at the end of the block. Would their treasure be buried in the same spot? Was this a race with only one treasure, or would they both find treasure?

There wasn't time to find out. Their first clue was at the garage. "Corned beef and cabbage—a St. Patrick's Day meal." What could that mean? The next stop on their map looked like a rectangle. "Corned beef...rectangle... let's see...I know! I bet that's a restaurant!" Phil declared. "But there's no restaurant around here," Sam began, when simultaneously they all said, "B and J's ice cream!" Off they went to the next block where Mr. and Mrs. Sanders sold ice cream in the summer time.

Sure enough! A green balloon floated above the bushes near the sidewalk. "Treasure clue" was printed on it. The boys popped the balloon and found another cryptic message written in green letters: "A shamrock has three." Three leaves, of course, the boys thought. They looked at the map. Sure enough, the next spot looked like a cluster of green trees. But which trees? The map showed a westerly direction, and Patrick said, "This way, guys!"

The game went on for quite some time. The boys were on their last clue, when they saw the other team heading toward the McCabes' backyard. Both groups converged on the sandbox that hadn't been used since last summer. It was obvious something had been buried very recently in the sand—probably after the boys left on their hunt.

"The treasure's here!" the boys called, and they quickly found two plastic containers labeled "Team One" and "Team Two" in green permanent marker.

Opening the containers, each team discovered a golden pot inside. Ignoring their dirty hands, the team leaders dug into the golden pots. Inside were movie tickets—enough for everyone. Everyone was excited. "What a great treasure!" "We're rich!" "What movie do you wanna see?" "These tickets are for a really good theater."

Finally the ice cream and cake had been eaten, and the last boy had said, "Thanks, Mr. McCabe. Thanks, Patrick." Patrick's dad gave his son a friendly little punch. "Hey, Patrick, what would you like to do next year on your birthday?"

Without hesitation, Patrick answered, "Another treasure hunt!"

■ ■ ■

Understanding the Story

1. Why did Patrick McCabe think he had luck?

2. What treasure did the boys find?

3. Do you think you would enjoy a treasure hunt? What treasure would you like to find?

Suggested Activities

1. Have your own treasure hunt. Challenge your learners to find the treasures you have hidden in the classroom or meeting space.

2. Invite each of the learners to draw a map on ways to reach heaven.

3. Dramatize the parable of the treasure hidden in the field.

4. Ask the children: If you were stranded on an island, which seven things would you want with you? Why?

Gardenia's Garden

The most important story in the Bible is the story of Jesus' resurrection. If Jesus had not risen from the tomb, we would not believe that he is God. We would not be following his words and we would not be trying to live as he did. He would have been just like every other human being who dies. The Resurrection proved that he is God. The Resurrection also allowed Jesus to stay with us in a new way—through his Body and Blood and through his Spirit. Listen to the story of Jesus rising from the dead. Compare it to the story of "Gardenia's Garden."

The Scripture Reading

After the sabbath, as the first day of the week was dawning, Mary Magdalene and the other Mary went to see the tomb. And suddenly there was a great earthquake; for an angel of the Lord, descending from heaven, came and rolled back the stone and sat on it. His appearance was like lightning, and his clothing white as snow. For fear of him the guards shook and became like dead men. But the angel said to the women, "Do not be afraid; I know that you are looking for Jesus who was crucified. He is not here; for he has been raised, as he said. Come, see the place where he lay. Then go quickly and tell his disciples, 'He has been raised from the dead, and indeed he is going ahead of you to Galilee; there you will see him.' This is my message for you." So they left the tomb quickly with fear and great joy, and ran to tell his disciples. Suddenly Jesus met them and said, "Greetings!" And they came to him, took hold of his feet, and worshiped him. Then Jesus said to them, "Do not be afraid; go and tell my brothers to go to Galilee; there they will see me." (Matthew 28:1–10)

Understanding the Bible Story

1. On what day of the week did the women go to the tomb?

2. What happened as the angel appeared?

3. What did the risen Lord look like?

4. How did the guards react to the resurrection of Jesus?

5. Why did the angel say to the women, "Do not be frightened"?

6. What did the angel ask the women to do?

Meditation

Imagine that you are in a beautiful garden. This is the garden where Jesus was laid in a tomb on the day he died. You follow the path to the tomb and you are very surprised to see the stone rolled away. You look inside the tomb. (*pause*) At first you think someone stole the body of Jesus. When you leave the tomb to tell someone, your eyes are not used to the sunlight. You blink because the brilliant light is still dazzling your eyes. But it's not the sun! It's Jesus! Jesus has really risen from the dead. Tell Jesus how wonderful and amazing it is that he has risen from the tomb. Tell Jesus how much you love him and how glad you are that he is alive! (*Pause in silence.*)

GARDENIA'S GARDEN

Before reading the story have the children draw pictures of one part: storm, party, or garden. Sitting in order of the story, the children can show their pictures at the appropriate times.

Gardenia loved spring the best of all the seasons. Her birthday came during this season, and soon she would be two years old! Several other lambs had birthdays that week. It was lambing season—the time of year when many lambs are born. Some lambs were one year old, some were two years old, and some were just a day or two. You could easily spot the newest lambs. Their legs were wobbly, and they stayed close to their mothers.

For weeks Gardenia had been reminding her mother and father about her birthday. They assured her they would not forget, but Gardenia could not be too sure. Besides, she couldn't stop thinking of things she wanted for her birthday. Every day she added to her list.

Ever since she had turned one year old, Gardenia had wanted a garden all her own. And that was her birthday present! Her mother and father were giving her a plot of ground that would be all hers! Her father had turned up the earth and broken down the big clods of dirt. He put a little fence around the garden. All that was left to do was make some straight furrows for the seeds. Gardenia's mother had bought all kinds of seeds: carrots, green beans, peppers, sweet corn, tomatoes, and even three kinds of flowers. Daisies would make a lovely white border, xenias would add color, and marigolds would keep animals away. Gardenia could hardly wait for her birthday. Just two more nights!

On the night before her birthday Gardenia could hardly sleep. She tossed and turned on her bed of straw, which tickled her wool. Then lightning flashed, followed by thunder. Gardenia was not afraid. She thought, "The storm will soften the earth in my garden." She fell asleep thinking about her beautiful garden.

The next morning raindrops sparkled like shiny jewels on the twigs and branches. The sun peeked in the cracks of the barn wall and shone in Gardenia's eyes. As soon as she awoke, she remembered, "Today's my birthday! I'm two years old!"

Gardenia gamboled out of the barn with some of her friends. "Happy birthday, Gardenia!" they called. Gardenia's mother and father were standing near Gardenia's garden. "Happy birthday, dear!" they said and kissed her.

"Thanks, Mom! Thanks, Dad! My

Peppers

Cauliflower

Carrots

very own garden! This is the best birthday ever!"

"Here's your first present, dear," said her father. He handed her a long package. Gardenia untied the pink ribbon and tore off the silver paper. Inside was a set of gardening tools. She handled each one in anticipation. Oh, the wonderful things she would grow with her rake and hoe!

Then Gardenia's mother handed her a lovely basket with a big yellow bow. Inside were packets of seeds.

"May I plant these now?" Gardenia asked eagerly.

"Well, we better have breakfast first." Gardenia was disappointed. But her mother reminded her that the ground was still too damp from last night's storm. The lamb agreed to wait until that afternoon.

Gardenia gobbled down lunch. Then she ran as fast as her little legs could carry her. Her father was putting a string on a stick. He told her to walk with the string to the other end of the garden. With a straight string to mark the row, her father dug the first furrow. Finally there were ten very straight rows ready for seeds.

Gardenia tore open the package of carrot seeds. She was amazed at how small they were. "How could carrots ever grow from such small seeds?" she wondered. She read the directions carefully, then began to put the seeds into the ground. When the carrots were tucked inside the dirt, Gardenia took the pepper and tomato seedlings. She carefully placed the tiny plants into their holes. She left plenty of room, because she knew the peppers and tomatoes would become large plants. By this time Gardenia was becoming quite hot, and her legs were sore. She went to the trough to get some cold water and then sat for a while.

Her mother and father checked on her progress. "You've done a beautiful job of planting! We'll help you put the rest of the seeds into the ground tomorrow." Gardenia agreed. That night a very tired two-year-old lamb blew out the two candles on her birthday cake.

The next day all three sheep worked to finish the planting. Again Gardenia was so tired that she could hardly stay awake during supper. Later, tucked in her straw, Gardenia sleepily mumbled to her mother, "Tomorrow my garden will be so big. I'll have many things to pick." With that she fell asleep. She dreamed of bushel baskets of vegetables all from her very own garden.

Two days had gone by since her birthday. Gardenia was eager to see all the lovely flowers and vegetables. She looked out the barn door, but she didn't see anything except the sticks with the names of what she had planted in the rows: carrots, green beenz, corn, and flours. (Gardenia still had a lot to learn about spelling.) Bursting into tears, Gardenia stumbled toward her precious garden. Her mother caught up with her.

"Dear, why are you crying?"

"My garden did...didn't...grow!" Gardenia said between sobs. "Noth... ing...came...up!"

54

"Gardenia," her mother consoled, "seeds take a very long time to grow. This is only spring. We will need to wait until summer."

"But aren't the seeds doing anything?" Gardenia wondered.

"Of course, they're doing something! They're dying—" her mother began, but she was cut off by a loud wail from Gardenia.

"Dying! I want my seeds to live! I wanted to have nice things to eat and flowers to smell. Now you tell me my seeds are dying. Didn't I do it right? Daddy helped me." Gardenia could not understand what her mother was telling her. What good were seeds for a birthday present, if nothing would grow?

"Lambkin," her mother said endearingly, "all seeds die. That's how plants and flowers grow. You put the seeds into the ground where they split apart. That's called 'dying.' Dying is part of the seed's life. It's really quite powerful! Only in the dark earth, with rain and sunshine feeding them, can the wonderful thing called 'life' happen. Those tiny seeds hold some mighty large carrots and peppers and flowers. You'll see. Just wait."

Gardenia's mother was right. A week later tiny shoots appeared. "They're coming! They're coming!" Gardenia called. "I'm going to have a garden after all!"

After several more weeks Gardenia and her parents pulled up the first carrots. They were delicious! The lamb and her family watched the green beans and peppers get bigger. After a very long time the green tomatoes began to blush bits of red. All summer long Gardenia's family and friends enjoyed the flowers. Finally even the tomatoes were ripe for their first picking.

Gardenia thought, "What a wonderful thing a garden is! And to think the first step is dying!" Gardenia still found the idea of life coming from death very fascinating. She had always thought it was the other way around. Life first, then death. But no, it was death, then life. Spring really had a lot of mystery. Spring was very full of life.

Understanding the Story

1. What did Gardenia want for her birthday present?

2. What did she plant in her garden?

3. Does a plant need a long time to grow?

4. What do seeds need to do before they become plants?

5. What is a mystery? What was the mystery of spring that Gardenia learned?

6. What are the signs and symbols of new life in this story?

Suggested Activities

1. Have your learners plant some flower seeds or other seeds and watch them grow. They might use the flowers for Mother's Day gifts or for another special day.

2. The children might make a garden of paper flowers. Let some of the flowers represent the good things they know about themselves: kind, generous, obedient, and so on. Let others represent the good qualities they want to grow in.

3. Have an egg hunt for plastic eggs with pictures or symbols of the Christian faith inside. After the hunt, see how many symbols or pictures the learners recognize.

4. With your help, invite the children to decorate eggs, prepare baskets, and take or send them to children in a hospital.

Angels to the Rescue

ANGELS

PRAYER

MESSAGES

PROTECTION

Angels are spirits who serve God. We find them in Scripture bringing messages from God. For example, the angel Gabriel spoke to Zechariah to announce the birth of John the Baptist and visited Mary to announce the birth of Jesus. Angels were with Jesus during his earthly life, beginning at his birth when they announced the good news to the shepherds, until his agony in the garden when they ministered to him. Angels will be present when Christ returns again. God's angels watch over us and pray for all of us.

The Scripture Reading

I am going to send an angel in front of you, to guard you on the way and to bring you to the place that I have prepared. Be attentive to him and listen to his voice. (Exodus 23:20–21a)

Understanding the Bible Story

1. Can we see angels?

2. What role has God given angels to help us human beings?

3. How can we listen to the voices of angels?

4. What do you think angels will tell us?

5. Do you know other stories from the Bible about angels?

Meditation

Imagine that you are able to lie on a cloud. Imagine that your guardian angel is there, too. Your guardian angel says, "I give you messages from God. Today what message would you like to give to God?" Think what you'd like to tell God. (*pause*) Would you like to ask God for help? Does someone in your family, school, or neighborhood need God's help? (*pause*) Do you want to thank God for all God's gifts? Do you want to tell God that creation is beautiful? Take some time now to give the angel your message to God. (*Pause in silence.*)

ANGELS TO THE RESCUE

Jerry and Carrie were twins. They both had red hair that hung in their eyes, freckles that increased in the summer sun, and long legs that let them run fast. They also were full of mischief. Together they would concoct wild schemes that often put them in danger. Fortunately they also had guardian angels to take care of them. Arnie Angel took care of Jerry, and Angie Angel took care of Carrie.

When Jerry and Carrie were infants, they decided they wanted to get out of their crib. But, as always, the sides of the crib were up. Together they managed to form a little ramp. They climbed up and plopped out the other side, landing on their parents' bed. What fun! What freedom! Little did they know that Arnie and Angie saw what was coming and pushed the parents' bed close to the crib. Arnie and Angie were so proud of their life-saving skills that they gave each other a high five and praised the Lord. From that moment on Arnie and Angie increased their prayers for Jerry and Carrie. "Dear God, don't let the twins be so hyper!" they pleaded.

On one particular day when Jerry and Carrie were eight years old, they were waiting for the school bus. They saw the red lights of the bus as it stopped to pick up a neighbor. Suddenly Jerry realized that he had forgotten his lunch. He ran back toward the house, and Carrie ran after him, yelling, "You'll miss the bus. I can give you some of my lunch." Just as she was saying this, they heard

the screech of tires and a big crunch. Looking around, they saw a car and a bent mailbox right where they had been standing. If Jerry hadn't forgotten his lunch, the twins would have been injured or killed.

Above them Angie and Arnie gave each other the thumbs-up. This was another time they had come to the rescue. Angie complimented Arnie: "Good work on hiding that lunch, then letting Jerry suddenly remember!"

"Let's praise the Lord!" Arnie reminded her.

Life went on. Arnie flew on his holy-esther wings to prevent Jerry from falling into the lake when he fished for blue gills. Angie would help Carrie think of ways to make new friends. Both angels sent the twins little messages like, "Pick up your clothes" and "Be kind to your classmates" and "Don't forget your prayers."

Carrie and Jerry grew, too. Most of the time they never thought about their guardian angels except when their teachers or parents asked them to pray the Angel Prayer. "Angel of God, my guardian dear" they would begin. Then Arnie and Angie would beam with pleasure. They weren't forgotten! They were being appreciated! As soon as the prayer was finished, the twins offered the prayer to God.

God was the one who received all the prayers. God gave the angels their duties. "Okay, Arnie and Angie, you heard the prayers from the twins. Now go forth and continue to protect them and give them messages from me."

For the next few years Angie and Arnie took care that Carrie didn't fall during cross country meets and that Jerry didn't tear a ligament during basketball practice.

The angels are still protecting the twins. They are still giving them messages from God. The only difference is that now the twins have grown. The two are closer to God, and they thank God for the angels who help them on their journey.

◼ ◼ ◼

Understanding the Story

1. How did the angels protect the twins?

2. Did you ever feel the protection of your guardian angels? Did you ever have a close call but escaped injury?

3. Do you pray for the help of your guardian angel? Do you honor them on their feast days?

Suggested Activities

1. Memorize a prayer to your guardian angel, if you don't know one by heart.

2. Create a skit with a guardian angel helping children.

3. Make up a word search using words about angels from Scripture and from the teaching of the church.

4. Write a commercial for television. In it remind people to pray to their guardian angels.